ENERGY SOURCES

Biofuels

by Tracy Vonder Brink

A Crabtree Crown Book

CRABTREE
Publishing Company
www.crabtreebooks.com

School-to-Home Support for Caregivers and Teachers

This appealing book is designed to teach students about core subject areas. Students will build upon what they already know about the subject, and engage in topics that they want to learn more about. Here are a few guiding questions to help readers build their comprehension skills. Possible answers appear here in red.

Before Reading:

What do I know about biofuels?

- *I know fuel makes energy.*
- *I know fuel runs cars.*

What do I want to learn about this topic?

- *I want to know about different kinds of biofuels.*
- *I want to learn how biofuels are made.*

During Reading:

I'm curious to know...

- *I'm curious to know which biofuel is used in cars.*
- *I'm curious to know which biofuel is used in trucks.*

How is this like something I already know?

- *I know gasoline is used in cars.*
- *I know diesel fuel is used in trucks.*

After Reading:

What was the author trying to teach me?

- *The author was trying to teach me what biofuels are.*
- *The author was trying to teach me how biofuels can replace fossil fuels.*

How did the photographs and captions help me understand more?

- *The photographs helped me understand how biofuels are made.*
- *The captions gave me extra information.*

Table of Contents

Chapter 1

Energy and Fuel 4

Chapter 2

What Are Biofuels? 10

Chapter 3

What Is Ethanol? 12

Chapter 4

What Is Biodiesel? 16

Chapter 5

What Is Biogas? 20

Chapter 6

Possible Biofuels 23

Chapter 7

The Future of Biofuels 27

Glossary 30

Index 31

Comprehension Questions 31

About the Author 32

Chapter 1: Energy and Fuel

We need energy for everything we do. Energy heats our homes. Our bodies use it to live. It fuels our cars. But what is energy?

In science, work is energy moving from one object to another. Your feet pushing against your bike's pedals are doing work that makes the bike move.

Energy is the ability of something to do work, or to make something happen. Energy is everywhere. It comes in different forms. Heat, light, and sound are all forms of energy. The lights in your home use electrical energy.

Transforming Energy

Energy can be transformed, or changed, from one form to another. Energy changes forms when it is used to make something happen. Wood has energy locked inside it. Burning the wood changes its energy into heat and light.

Heat and light are two forms of energy.

A fuel is something that is changed in some way to produce energy. Wood is a fuel because burning it releases heat and light. Food is fuel for your body. Your body breaks down what you eat and uses it as energy.

Fossil Fuels

Fossil fuels are nonrenewable energy sources. Nonrenewable means they cannot be replaced.

We use fuels to make heat and power. Coal, oil, and natural gas are fuels. They are burned to release their energy. They all come from underneath the ground and they formed over millions of years. These types of fuels are called fossil fuels. If we use them up, they cannot be replaced.

Climate Change

Fossil fuels give off **carbon dioxide** when they are burned. Carbon dioxide collects in a layer around Earth. This layer traps heat and warms the planet. As Earth becomes warmer, its **climate** changes. We need energy sources that will not run out and that will not change the climate. We need **alternative** sources of energy. One such source is biofuels.

Climate change harms people and animals. Impacts of climate change include higher temperatures and changes in rainfall. This can lead to wildfires and less water for crops. These changes affect where people and animals live and the food that they eat.

Biomass

Plants turn sunlight into the energy that they need to live. They also store energy. Biomass is plant material that can be changed into fuel. Biomass may be crops or leftover parts of crops, such as corncobs. It may be grasses. Wood and wood waste such as sawdust or wood chips may also be biomass.

Biofuels

Biomass is a source of biofuel. For example, corn is biomass. It can be made into ethanol, a biofuel. Biofuels may be used instead of fossil fuels.

Plants for Ethanol

Ethanol may be used with gasoline to fuel cars. As well as corn, ethanol can also be made from crops such as sugarcane and sugar beets. Grasses, trees, and leftover parts of plants may also be used in ethanol. In the United States, ethanol is most often made from corn.

The United States uses corn to make ethanol because it already grows a lot of the crop. Corn is also often cheaper than other types of biomass.

Grain sorghum, corn, and sugarcane may all be made into ethanol.

How Corn Becomes Fuel

Other kinds of plants go through the same steps as corn to become ethanol. Brazil makes most of its ethanol from sugarcane.

The first step in changing corn into ethanol is to grind it. Water and ingredients that will help change the corn are added. The mixture is heated. The corn releases sugars. **Yeast** goes in next. The yeast eats the sugars and produces ethanol.

Using Ethanol

Cars can have as few as four spark plugs, or as many as 16.

How do cars run on ethanol? Usually, cars burn gasoline and air. The spark plugs in a car's engine light this mix and make it explode. The small explosions move rods that turn the wheels. Ethanol burns the same way, but it is often blended with gasoline because cars run best on gas.

Today, most fuel sold at gas stations is a blend of gasoline and ethanol. Blends that have lower amounts of ethanol can power all cars. Some blends have higher amounts, but cars need special engines to use them.

Biodiesel is a liquid fuel made from vegetable oil or animal fats. Vegetable oil comes from crops such as canola, sunflower, and soybean. The seeds are cleaned, ground up, and heated. A machine presses them and squeezes out the oil.

How Vegetable Oil Becomes Fuel

The thickener from vegetable oil can be used to make soap. It can also be used in lotions.

Vegetable oil contains a natural **thickener**. The thickener must be removed before the oil can be used as a fuel. Alcohol and ingredients that help separate the oil are added. Everything is heated and mixed. The oil and the thickener separate. The biodiesel is skimmed off and cleaned.

Using Biodiesel

Cars that run on used cooking oil may smell like the food that was cooked in it. Some of these cars smell like french fries!

Biodiesel can also be made from used cooking oil and grease from restaurants. The steps are the same as vegetable oil, except used oil must be cleaned well first. Used cooking oil also has more fat in it, which makes it take longer to remove the thickener.

All leftover food bits must be removed from used cooking oil before it is made into fuel.

Oil heaters fueled by diesel may also use a biodiesel blend instead.

Trucks and other large vehicles use diesel, which is a fossil fuel. Trucks run best on diesel fuel. So, biodiesel is blended with diesel. Most trucks and large vehicles can use these blends.

Biogas may be captured from **landfills**. It comes from garbage. Trash goes into a landfill and is covered with soil. **Bacteria** live in the waste and dirt. The bacteria break down the garbage. As the garbage rots, it releases gas. Landfills have a system that captures this gas.

Biogas captured from landfills is treated and cleaned. It is burned to produce energy.

Some sewage treatment plants can also capture biogas. Poop flushed down the toilet goes to a treatment plant. The same bacteria that breaks down garbage also works on poop.

Some heating systems and stoves burn natural gas. Biogas may be used instead. It can also be changed into a form of fuel for cars and trucks. However, most vehicles do not have biogas engines.

A biogas plant in Denmark provides heat for about 57,000 homes.

Hydrogen Gas

Hydrogen is the most common **element** in the universe. It will never run out. Hydrogen gas does not give off carbon dioxide when it is burned. Some fuel cells and batteries are made to run on hydrogen gas.

Hydrogen gas is usually made by splitting water with electricity. Scientists are working on ways to change biomass and waste into hydrogen gas. Using garbage to create hydrogen gas could get rid of trash and provide a lasting energy source. But right now, hydrogen fuel cells are very expensive.

About 3 percent of buses in the United States use hydrogen fuel cells.

Hydrogen
FUEL CELL BUS

H2

Algae

Algae are simple plants with no leaves or stems.
They grow on or near water in many places.
Algae grow faster than other kinds of plants.
This could make algae a good source of biofuel.

Scientists are working on ways to change algae to biofuel. It is expensive though, and growing algae and changing it to biofuel takes a lot of water. However, algae may be a promising energy source in the future.

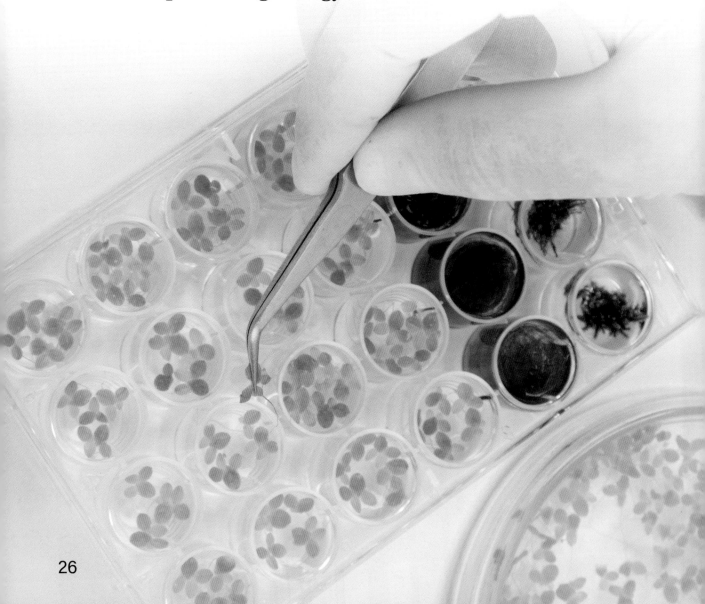

Chapter 7: The Future of Biofuels

Biofuels burn more cleanly than fossil fuels, but they still give off carbon dioxide. However, plants take carbon dioxide out of the air as they grow. When crops are planted to replace the ones used in biofuel, new plants remove carbon dioxide from the air.

Reaching a balance between the amount of carbon dioxide put into the air with the amount taken out is called net zero.

The United States would need to plant millions of acres of corn to grow enough to fuel all of its cars with ethanol alone.

Relying on ethanol and biodiesel as our only fuels could cause problems. We would need lots of land to grow enough plants. Growing a lot of crops takes a lot of water. Using crops for fuel might mean less food for people and animals.

Biofuels reduce carbon dioxide. They work in today's vehicles. They will not run out. Biofuels are not the perfect solution for climate change, but they help. Will biofuels help even more in the future?

Glossary

alternative (ahl-TUR-nuh-tive): Something that may be chosen instead of something else

bacteria (bak-TEE-ree-uh): Small organisms, or living things, that can be found in all natural environments

carbon dioxide (CAR-bun dye-OX-ide): A gas that is produced when people or animals breathe out or when certain fuels are burned

climate (KLEYE-muht): The usual weather conditions of a particular place

element (EH-luh-muhnt): A pure substance made from a single type of atom

landfills (LAND-filz): Areas where waste is buried under the ground

thickener (THIK-uh-ner): A substance that makes a liquid firmer or more solid

yeast (YEEST): A tiny single-celled organism often used in baking

Index

biomass 10-12, 24
carbon dioxide 9, 23, 27, 29
corn 11-13, 28
energy 4-10, 20, 24, 26
fossil fuel(s) 8-11, 19, 27

garbage 20-21, 24
gasoline 12, 14-15
hydrogen 23-24
plants 10, 12, 25, 27, 28
vegetable oil 16-17

Comprehension Questions

1. What is biomass?
   a. A type of fossil fuel
   b. Bacteria that live in waste and dirt
   c. Plant material that can be changed into fuel

2. Which biofuel is blended with gasoline to fuel cars?
   a. Algae
   b. Hydrogen gas
   c. Ethanol

3. What can be used used to make biodiesel?
   a. Vegetable oil
   b. Ethanol
   c. Garbage

4. True or False: Nonrenewable energy sources can be replaced.

5. True or False: Biogas can be made from rotting garbage.

Comprehension questions answer key: 1. c 2. c 3. a 4. False 5. True

Tracy Vonder Brink loves true stories and facts. She has written more than 20 books for kids and is a contributing editor for three children's science magazines. Tracy lives in Cincinnati, Ohio, with her husband, two daughters, and two rescue dogs.

CRABTREE
Publishing Company

Written by: Tracy Vonder Brink
Designed by: Jennifer Bowers
Series Development: James Earley
Proofreader: Melissa Boyce
Educational Consultant: Marie Lemke M.Ed.
Print Coordinator: Katherine Berti

Photographs: cover and p.12 ©2021 Mabeline72/Shutterstock, ©2016 Aedka Studio/Shutterstock, ©2016 jeep2499/Shutterstock, ©R2D2/Shutterstock; p.4 ©2021 Lin Xiu Xiu/Shutterstock; p.5 ©2015 Africa Studio/Shutterstock; p.6 ©2020 Natalia Leinonen/Shutterstock; p.7 ©2016 Tatjana Baibakova/Shutterstock; p8. ©2020 Sunshine Seeds/Shutterstock; p.9 ©2009 Mark Smith/Shutterstock; p.10 ©2015 nostal6ie/Shutterstock; p.11 ©2021 Scharfsinn/Shutterstock; p.13 ©2021 ThamKC/Shutterstock; p.14 ©2019 Ted PAGEL/Shutterstock; p.15 ©2017 jaboo2foto/Shutterstock; p.16 ©2020 Photoagriculture/Shutterstock; p.17 ©2018 chakapong/Shutterstock; p.18 ©2017 Mama Belle and the kids/Shutterstock; p.19 ©2017 Carolyn Franks/Shutterstock; p.20 ©2018 newphotoservice/Shutterstock; p.21 ©2015 Belish/Shutterstock; p.22 ©2018 Coral Mint Stock/Shutterstock; p.23 ©2015 Takashi Images/Shutterstock; p.24 ©2021 Scharfsinn/Shutterstock; p.25 ©2019 Chokniti Khongchum/Shutterstock; p.26 ©2020 Tonhom1009/Shutterstock; p.27 ©2017 muratart/Shutterstock; p.28 ©2013 B Brown/Shutterstock; p.29 ©2015 Gleb Predko/Shutterstock

Library and Archives Canada Cataloguing in Publication

Available at the Library and Archives Canada

Library of Congress Cataloging-in-Publication Data

Available at the Library of Congress

Crabtree Publishing Company
www.crabtreebooks.com   1-800-387-7650

Published in the United States
Crabtree Publishing
347 Fifth Avenue
Suite 1402-145
New York, NY, 10016

Published in Canada
Crabtree Publishing
616 Welland Ave.
St. Catharines, ON
L2M 5V6

Printed in the U.S.A./072022/CG20220201